LITTLE WANDERERS

LITTLE WANDERERS

BY

MARGARET WARNER MORLEY

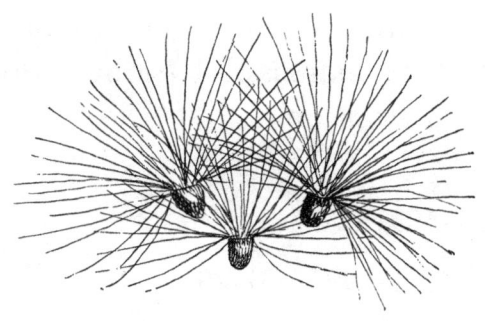

YESTERDAY'S CLASSICS
CHAPEL HILL, NORTH CAROLINA

Cover and arrangement © 2009 Yesterday's Classics, LLC.

This edition, first published in 2009 by Yesterday's Classics, an imprint of Yesterday's Classics, LLC, is an unabridged republication of the text originally published by Ginn and Company in 1900. For the complete listing of the books that are published by Yesterday's Classics, please visit www.yesterdaysclassics.com. Yesterday's Classics is the publishing arm of the Baldwin Online Children's Literature Project which presents the complete text of hundreds of classic books for children at www.mainlesson.com.

ISBN-10: 1-59915-317-3

ISBN-13: 978-1-59915-317-9

Yesterday's Classics, LLC
PO Box 3418
Chapel Hill, NC 27515

CONTENTS

Why Plants Travel 1
Those that Fly with Plumes or Down 4
    Dandelions 4
    Thistles 14
    Milkweeds 19
    Lettuce 23
    Clematis 25
    Asters and Golden-Rod 27
    The Willow 29
    Cattails 35
    Geraniums 37
    Cotton 39
    Other Fly-Aways 43

SEEDS THAT FLY WITH WINGS 45

    MAPLES. 45

    ELMS 49

    ASH TREES 51

    PINES 53

SEEDS THAT FLY WITHOUT WINGS
    OR PLUMES 56

OTHER SEEDS THAT ARE MOVED
    BY THE WIND 58

    TUMBLEWEEDS. 60

WANDERERS THAT CLING 62

    BURDOCKS 62

    COCKLEBURS AND SAND SPURS. 65

    TICK TREFOIL. 67

    STICK-TIGHTS 70

    AGRIMONY AND OTHER WEEDS 73

    FLAX 75

    MISTLETOE. 77

    OTHER PLANTS WITH STICKY SEEDS
        OR SEED PODS. 79

- Wanderers that Float 81
- Seeds that Animals Like to Eat 84
  - The Hickory 84
  - Walnuts and Butternuts 87
  - The Chestnut 89
  - Other Edible Seeds 91
  - Berries 93
  - Cherries 95
  - Apples 97
- Seeds that are Shot away 99
  - Oxalis 99
  - Witch-Hazel 101
  - Touch-Me-Not 103

WHY PLANTS TRAVEL

Plants are great travelers; they often wander far and wide. Sometimes they even cross the ocean and take up their abode in a new land.

The oxeye daisy, our common meadow buttercup, and the little Canada thistle, now so abundant everywhere, are not native Americans, but came here from Europe.

Very likely they sailed in the ships with the early settlers and took possession of the New World with them. They are so much at home now that most people think they always grew here. But they did not, and when the Pilgrim Fathers looked over their new home the fields were not white with daisies nor yellow with buttercups.

Buttercups

No doubt the Pilgrim Fathers were glad of this, for daisies and buttercups often cover the fields and spoil the hay, and while "daisies in the meadow" seem very lovely to the city people who go to the country for the summer, daisies in the hay are another matter, and the farmers do not think them lovely at all.

It is not the grown-up plants that travel, as a rule, though some of them do. For you must know the plant world is a topsy-turvy kind of place where the parents stand still at home and the children wander about.

Of course the children are the seeds, and they are free, but when they once settle down and begin to grow their wandering days are over.

Plants with roots are great home-bodies; nothing short of actual violence can make them move from the spot they have chosen. Frequently it happens that they die if moved.

Not so with the seeds, however.

They wander about, and their parents often take great pains to send them out into the world.

For the children of the plants are very apt to die if they remain at home too long. They need to find a place in which to settle down and grow, and it is often better for them to do this at a distance from their parents.

Plants eat what is in the soil, and each kind of plant needs some particular earth food. When plants of one kind are crowded too closely in a place the earth is often impoverished, and the plant might die out if it were not able to find a fresh growing place. Then, again, if the seeds always fell close to the parent plant, the earth would soon become too crowded to support more than a very few new plants.

So for these and other reasons it is best for the seeds to go while they are able and find a place for themselves.

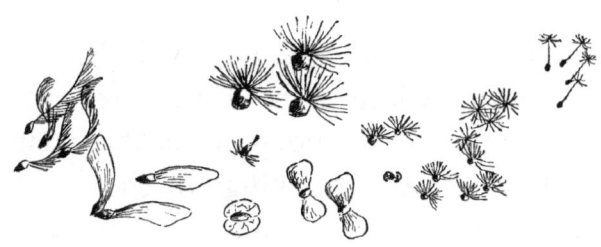

Some happy wanderers

Nearly all seeds are provided with some way of moving about, and while some of them go very short distances others go very long ones.

They travel for their profit, and why may we not say for their pleasure? For if a plant is able to feel and enjoy at all,—and I for one believe it is,—then the dandelion seeds must feel very joyous sailing before the wind in the early summer, and later the thistle-down and the milkweed seeds, scudding before the breeze.

THOSE THAT FLY WITH PLUMES OR DOWN

DANDELIONS

EVERYBODY is well acquainted with the dandelion, but not everybody knows that it was brought to this country from Europe. It is not probable that a dandelion seed could come on the wings of the wind three thousand miles across nor is it probable that people would bring it on purpose.

Very likely dandelion seeds were accidentally mixed with the grass and clover seeds brought from their homes in the Old World.

Before the coming of the white man the Indian did not see the roadsides yellow with dandelions, nor did he see dandelions at all, excepting a kind that grows sparingly way up north and another that grows in the Rocky Mountains.

The European dandelions liked the New World and when they had the chance spread very fast, so that now they are everywhere—at least in the East.

The reason they were able to spread so is that the dandelion seeds were able to fly.

If they had not flown away but had dropped down close to the parent plant and grown there, they would not have been allowed to spread much; for people do not like dandelions in their fields and lawns, and try hard to root them out.

This would be easy if the dandelions kept together in patches. But they seem to say "catch me if you can" as they fly on the wings of the wind, dropping down here, there, and everywhere, striking root and merrily growing.

The parent dandelion takes very good care of its seed children, and plans for their future success by

White-headed dandelions

LITTLE WANDERERS

giving each one a little plume by which it can be blown about by the wind.

Everybody knows the pretty, fluffy, white-headed dandelions that come after the yellow flowers.

Children often blow on them "to see what time it is." If all the seeds fly away but one, they say it is one o'clock; if two remain, they say it is two o'clock, and so on.

Seed case and plume magnified

They also blow on them to see if "mother wants me," as every child knows.

Each little silky part that flies away is a seed case and its plume.

If you look carefully at the part of the dandelion that flies about, you will see the little brown seed case at one end, shaped something like a tiny cucumber, and with little teeth near its top.

Out of its top grows a silky white stalk, and at the end of this is a tuft of soft little hairs by means of which the seed case can float in the air.

The flat cushion with a few seeds attached

Each dandelion seed case contains one little seed, but the case fits the seed so closely that most people speak of the whole thing—seed case and seed together—as the seed. The proper name for such a seed case and its seed is akene.[1] Not all akenes have plumes.

---

[1] à-kēn′

DANDELIONS

The top of the dandelion stem is a flat cushion, and the little akenes, when the seeds are ripe, stand on it, pointing out in different directions so there may be room for every one with its spread-out plume.

The plumes do not open out until the seed is ready to be blown away, and the akenes do not stand pointing out in all directions until the time to fly has come. Before that they are all packed closely together.

Before the plume opens out

All closely packed together

Because the little akene is so light and feathery the breeze bears it along, sometimes for quite a distance, but at last it drops down to the earth or else is blown among the grasses or weeds or stones and lodges there, and when the right time comes the seed that is in the little brown seed case sprouts.

Sometimes the air seems to be full of dandelion akenes floating about.

Although the dandelion is so bright and pretty, people do not like it in their lawns.

Excepting when in bloom or when it is "white-headed," it is not as pretty as grass. It does not make a beautiful velvety carpet to the earth, but its leaves look ragged and uneven and spoil the appearance of the lawn.

It is from its leaves that the dandelion gets its name, for "dandelion" means "tooth of a lion"; and if you look at a well-grown dandelion leaf you will understand why it came to have such a fierce name.

Dandelions are very fond of growing in lawns. They

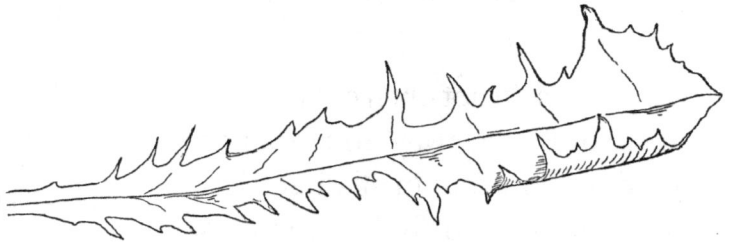

A well-grown dandelion leaf

like to be taken care of, and they seem to like to have their heads cut off.

Anyway the lawn mower does not trouble them in the least.

Their leaves grow close to the ground, in the shape of a rosette, and when the lawn mower passes over, only the large outer leaves are harmed; the young ones towards the center of the rosette remain unhurt and have more light and air and space to grow in; so our dandelion flourishes in spite of its pruning.

When a dandelion once gets its roots started it does not make so very much difference if it has its flowers cut off, for it does not die when winter comes. Only its leaves die. Its root continues alive in the earth, and in the spring wakes up and puts out new leaves.

So cutting off the flowers does not destroy the dandelion, it merely prevents seeds from forming, and more dandelions from starting.

DANDELIONS

Dandelion roots kill the grass by pushing it aside and taking the earth-food for themselves.

So if dandelions get started in a lawn they will soon kill out the grass, and then there will be a dandelion lawn instead of a grass lawn!

A dandelion lawn is very beautiful for a little while in the early summer. Sometimes it looks like a carpet of gold, the yellow flowers are so thick and fine. But when they are done blossoming the lawn is a sorry looking sight.

Dandelions do not trouble the hay fields, for where the grass is allowed to grow tall it soon smothers them.

Boys are often hired to dig dandelion roots out of lawns, and near large cities poor women may often be seen digging them out for the sake of the young leaves which, when they first come up in the spring, make very good "greens." These people sell them or eat them instead of spinach. Tender young dandelion leaves are very good indeed, and some people like them better than spinach.

Dandelion plants have a wise way of protecting their seed children until the time for flight.

The flower buds come out of the center of the leaf rosette, close to the ground. They have very short stems and seem to sit right on the rosette.

There are a great many flowers in one dandelion head.

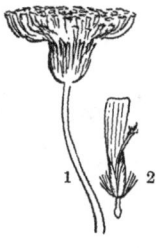

1. A cluster of flowers.
2. One flower magnified

Each little yellow part of the dandelion flower head is a separate blossom, and each separate blossom has one seed case with a seed inside growing to the bottom of it.

All of these blossoms are shut up at first in a case of green, leaf-like parts, and form the bud.

As the bud grows older its stem lengthens a little, as you can see in the picture on page 9—unless it is on a lawn. Then it does not lengthen; it seems to know the lawn mower will come along and take off its head if it grows taller, so it stays close to the ground. After a while the

The bud

green bud opens, the many little yellow flowers push their way out, and the dandelion is in bloom.

Towards night the dandelion shuts up again; the tiny yellow flowers press close together, and the outer covering of green bracts, as they are called, closes up, too, and shuts them in all snug and safe.

When the dandelion has once closed it does not open again. But its stem, which was very short, begins to lengthen.

It is a hollow stem, as you know, and has a bitter, milky juice.

Longer and longer grows the stem with the closed-up flower cluster at its top. But this wise stem does not stand up. Oh, no, indeed! it lies down or leans over, concealed by the grass and weeds, unless it grows on a lawn. Then the wise stem does not lengthen much; it is afraid of that lawn mower.

If the dandelion is growing among tall grass, the stem will grow very long indeed; if among short grass it will not grow so long.

By this time you can guess why. When the seeds are ripe and the silky plumes all nicely formed that stem stands up!

It stands straight up and looks over the tops of the grasses. Then the green bracts on the outside turn back, and the silky tufts spread out and pull themselves free from the remains of the tiny flowers which have withered and are no longer yellow. They do not fall off when the flower first closes, but make a little cap to protect the growing akenes, and when these get ready to open out the cap is pushed off by them.

LITTLE WANDERERS

The hollow stem stands up, and its lovely silky head of plumed akenes shines in the sunlight.

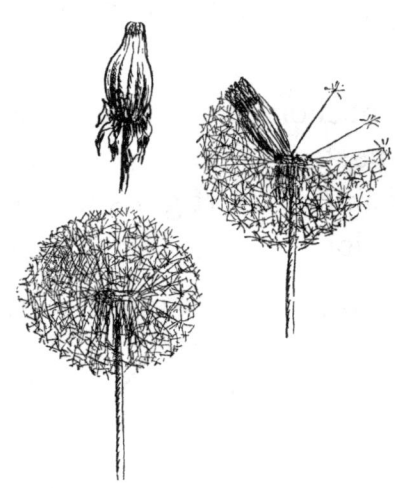

Opening out and pushing off the cap

There is nothing much prettier in the plant world than this head of fairy dandelion akenes all ready to fly away.

They stand and shine until a breeze comes along that is strong enough to dislodge them, then all in a moment they are off sailing through the air.

The parent plant is not sorry to have them go, for this is what it has worked so hard to accomplish; and as they float away, if it thinks at all, it no doubt hopes that each little shining wanderer will alight at last in a beautiful home of its own with plenty of space and sunlight and food for its growth.

If there is not breeze enough to carry away the dandelion akenes, when night approaches or a storm gathers the careful parent plant does not allow these silky treasures to become soaked and spoiled by moisture.

Each little plume shuts up again! The silky tufts no longer spread out, and the green bracts, too, turn up and cover them safely as before. They go to sleep, hoping, no doubt, for better luck next day.

DANDELIONS

There is no better fun than to watch the dandelions do these things.

When children blow the heads of dandelions away, that is just what the dandelions want, for it sets all the akenes flying about in the air above the earth.

The main thing for a dandelion seed is to get started. If it can get up in the air free from the weeds and grasses, it will be sure to take quite a journey and will doubtless settle in a new home.

The bitter milky juice of the dandelion very likely protects it from being eaten by various plant-eating creatures.

This juice is familiar to country children who pick the long stems of the dandelions, split them, and "curl" the parts in their mouths.

These pretty stems make very long and fine curls, as every little country girl knows.

THISTLES

Nobody can help liking thistles—that is, to look at. We do not care to handle them, nor do they care to have us, which perhaps is why they are covered all over with such sharp prickles.

The prickles are an intimation to us to let them alone.

They do not want to be handled, and they do not want to be eaten. When a plant arms itself with thorns or prickles, that is its way of saying "hands off." Few creatures besides donkeys eat thistles.

It is said that donkeys are fond of them, and some horses will nibble at them, but on the whole the thistles are let alone, excepting by the farmer, who digs them up.

Thistles are much more troublesome than dandelions, for they get into the hay and grain, and if let alone some kinds will kill out all other plants and occupy the land themselves.

There are many kinds of thistles. Our large native ones that bear beautiful showy purple, or pink, or white heads are not, as a rule, very troublesome to the farmer.

The little Canada thistle is the pest he dreads. That, like the dandelion, came from Europe. No doubt its seeds were first brought over—a very few of them—with other seeds from the Old World. But all the little emigrant asked was to get started.

Canada thistle

Once across the sea, it was able to conquer the plants of America and get a place for itself, for its seeds fly, like those of the dandelion, and in very much the same way.

The Canada thistle spreads by running roots that

live through the winter, as well as by seeds, so no wonder it quickly found its way far and wide.

It is for this reason sometimes called the creeping thistle, and because it is so troublesome it is also named the Cursed thistle.

There is a thistle in Europe which bears a light yellow flower head and is called the Blessed thistle or the Holy thistle. It has its name because people used to believe it had power to counteract poison. This thistle has been brought over from Europe, and is sometimes to be found in the southern part of the United States, where it has run wild.

Thistle heads are often very large and handsome. Like the dandelion flower clusters, they are made up of a large number of small blossoms.

Bees and butterflies are very fond of thistle honey, and they can almost always be found on the blossoms, sucking out the drop of honey which is to be found in each little flower of the cluster.

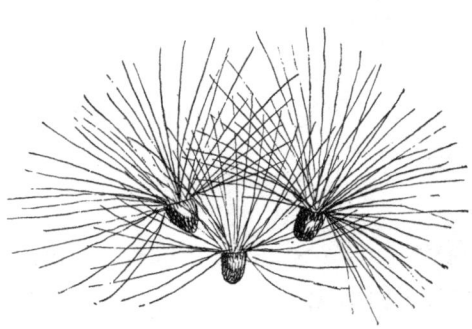

At the bottom of each little flower, as in the dandelion, is an akene. An akene, we remember, is a tight-fitting seed case containing one seed. The thistle akene also has a plume to fly with.

THISTLES

The thistle plume has no stalk, but grows right from the top of the akene. The plumed akenes are packed tightly away beneath the scaly bracts that surround them.

These bracts in the thistle are generally covered with sharp prickles. So, although one likes to look at a thistle and inhale its fragrance, it is not a pleasant flower to handle.

When the thistle seeds are ripe, the prickly covering loosens, and the akenes come trooping out in a soft, fluffy mass. Away they fly, one by one, as the breeze dislodges them and carries them off. They are much more showy than the dandelion akenes, for the plumes are much larger.

Away they go, this way and that, and after a while the wind blows them against a tree branch, or a fence rail, or a stone. Then the akene thus stopped drops off from the plume to the ground. The akene, in this case, is done sailing about. It has come to rest and very likely will lie until the next spring before it sprouts.

The plume is not harmed at all when the akene lets go, but at the next gust of wind flies on, lighter than ever.

One often sees these seedless plumes sailing about in the summer and fall.

LITTLE WANDERERS

People sometimes gather the heads of large thistles before the seeds are ripe, pull out the pink part of the flowers, carefully pull off the prickly bracts, and hang the rest up to dry. The akenes do not then fall off, but the plumy part fluffs out and makes a pretty pompon with which the children's hats can be trimmed.

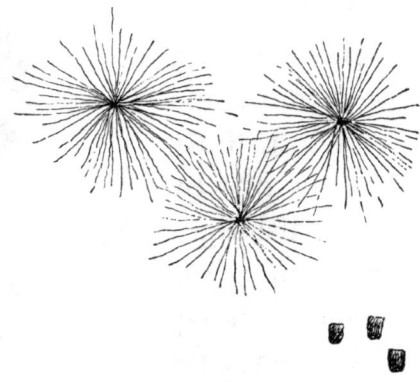

MILKWEEDS

Most of us like milkweeds. They are not so troublesome as the dandelions and thistles. They generally grow in waste places, along stone walls, or outside fences, where they do no harm to the crops but make the roadsides charming. Most kinds of milkweeds have a milky juice, as their name tells. It is thicker and stickier than the dandelion juice, and is very disagreeable if one gets it on his fingers.

This, no doubt, is why the plant makes it that way. It does not wish us to get its juice on our fingers; it wishes us to let it alone. It also wishes animals to let it alone and not eat it; and most animals are not fond of it. This is not true, however, of certain caterpillars.

LITTLE WANDERERS

Towards fall you will generally see the milkweed leaves covered with bright yellow and black caterpillars that certainly are lovely whether you think so or not.

If you take the largest of these caterpillars and put them in a box of earth with plenty of fresh milkweed leaves to eat as long as they want to eat (which will not be long), you will see what happens.

Something happens, and you will do well to find out about it.

Milkweeds have pretty, fragrant flowers that grow together, many in a bunch, but not close together into a solid head, like the little dandelion flowers. Each milkweed flower has its own little stem.

Not all of the flowers in a bunch of milkweed go to seed. Generally only one or two from each bunch do. The rest are crowded out and wither and fall off, for the milkweed flower develops a very large seed pod that holds a great many seeds, and there is not room on the stem for many of these big pods.

The flowers of our common milkweed are pink-purple in color, and the pods are fuzzy and irregular on the outside, and are shaped as you see in the picture.

Inside they are lovely. The pod itself is as smooth and

MILKWEEDS

shiny as satin, and there is a bridge running lengthwise; to this grow the seeds—a great many in each pod. Each seed has a plume and looks very much like the thistle akene with its plume. But these seeds have no seed case, excepting the large pod in which they all lie together. They grow inside this case, which opens to let them escape. The milkweed seed looks so much like the thistle akene that you would have to examine it very carefully to discover the difference.

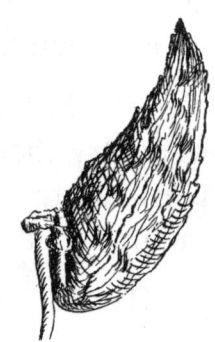

The milkweed seeds are brown and round and flat, and each has a silky plume, with no stalk to the plume. The seeds lie packed closely together in the pod with their plumes unopened, but when they are ripe the pod splits open down one side and the plumes fluff out.

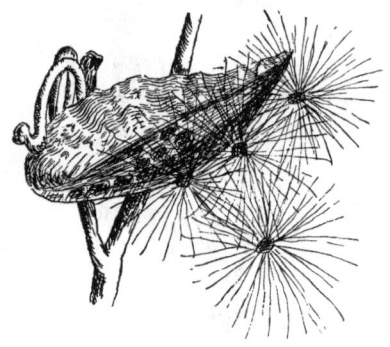

Then you will see a pretty sight. From the gap in the pod the pretty, silky seeds come spilling out. Their plumes touch each other and hold the seeds together in a soft feathery mass until along comes the breeze. Then one after another the pretty seeds float away and the empty pods are left behind.

Sometimes children catch bees in empty milkweed pods. The bees make a great buzzing in the pod, and it is not fair to keep them long, for it interferes with their honey-gathering or pollen-collecting. If there is anything a bee hates, it is to waste time, with so many hungry mouths at home waiting to be fed.

Like the thistles, when the milkweed seeds become quite dry they often drop away from their plumes, particularly if they strike against something when sailing about.

There are a number of species of milkweeds. One common species has bright, orange flowers, and is called butterfly weed. Its flowers look a little like bright butterflies, and the butterflies are fond of its honey.

There is a lovely milkweed in Florida that has large pea-green leaves with broad pink veins running all through them.

Some species of milkweeds have long, slender, smooth pods, and very likely you have noticed them along the roadside.

LETTUCE

THOSE who have seen lettuce only on the table, or growing in the early spring garden or in the green-house, will feel like laughing at the idea of lettuces flying!

Yet they do fly. At least their seeds do.

Sometimes lettuces look like rosettes growing out of the ground, and sometimes they look like little cabbages. But that is only the leaves.

If lettuces are let alone and not picked, in time they will "go to seed"; a stalk will grow up from the middle, with small leaves on it and a great many little flower heads that look somewhat like tiny dandelions.

Garden lettuce gone to seed

These flower heads are made like those of the dandelion or thistle.

The lettuce has no prickles, but its juice is milky and bitter, and gets more bitter as the plant grows older. The lettuce flowers have akenes like the dandelion, and each akene has a plume like that of the dandelion.

Away fly the pretty plumed akenes, and lettuce is thus sown by the wayside. But one seldom sees garden lettuce growing, except in gardens; for it is so tender the strong, rough weeds choke and kill it.

Wild lettuce

There is a wild lettuce, however, that has a large number of flower heads, and of course a great many pretty, silky, tufted akenes. These lettuces sometimes shine as if they had been snowed upon when their silky, white plumed akenes first open out.

I advise you to see if you can find some of them next summer. The best place to look is alongside fences and hedges and in the corners of pastures.

There is a lettuce so troublesome to the farmer that large sums of money have been appropriated to exterminate it. It is called the Prickly Lettuce, because its leaves and stalks are prickly. It came to this country from Europe. It is quite as destructive to the farmer's crops as is the Canada thistle.

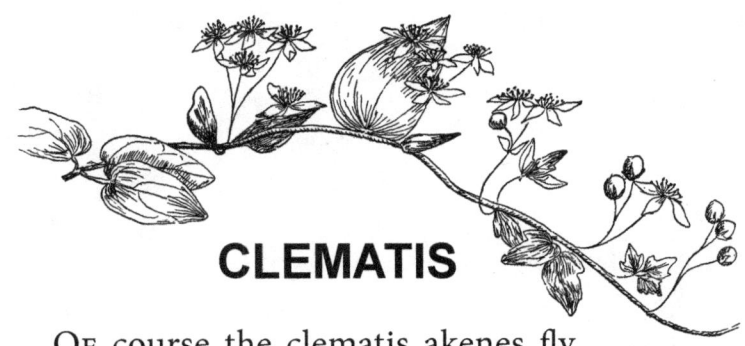

CLEMATIS

Of course the clematis akenes fly. Nothing so fluffy as they, in the seed world, could do otherwise.

The wild clematis that grows over the bushes in some swamps is a beautiful vine with glossy leaves and clusters of pretty white flowers. After the snowy flowers have gone it is still beautiful, for then each little akene waves a long, shining, curly plume. The whole vine is covered with these shining, twining plumes.

But a day comes when they no longer shine. Each curling plume looks like a mass of down, for its parts have separated and stand out, and we now see that it is shaped like a feather, a downy fluffy feather. The whole vine is a soft fluffy mass.

This does not last long, for the akenes leave the parent vine and are borne aloft on their airy plumes by the wind that scatters them far and wide.

Some fall upon the right kind of soil, where they are covered by the leaves of autumn, and lie safely until spring comes. Then they wake up and grow each into a beautiful clematis vine with shining leaves.

LITTLE WANDERERS

There is a beautiful clematis with large blue-purple flowers that grows in the mountains of Virginia and in some other places.

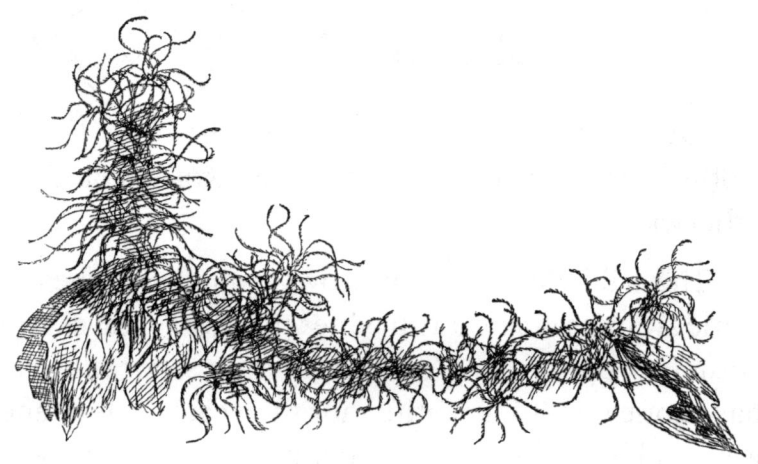

Clematis gone to seed

ASTERS AND GOLDEN-ROD

Asters and golden-rod blossom in the fall. Then the country roads are lovely to walk over, and the fields are as bright as can be with blue or purple or white asters and yellow golden-rod.

Some kinds of golden-rod and asters blossom in the summer, but most of them wait until late in the season. They are almost the last flowers to come and almost the last to go.

When their bright flowers fade they are still pretty. Each "flower" of the asters is like the dandelion, a cluster of very small flowers, and the golden-rod flower head is made up of very many tiny flowers.

Asters

Each little flower has its own akene and plume quite like the dandelion, but a great deal smaller, and in time the clusters that were flowers become clusters of soft downy plumes.

This state does not last long, for the akenes are

LITTLE WANDERERS

blown away by the wind and sown far and near over field and roadside.

If you brush against the downy aster and golden-rod heads when the seeds are ripe, the akenes will cling to your clothes like cobwebs and you will carry them about with you until finally they fall off.

Perhaps that is one way by which the golden-rod and aster seeds travel about; they cling to animals that pass and so are carried far away. But they do not cling as well as some other seeds we are soon to know about.

Golden-rod

THE WILLOW

THE willow that children know and love the best is the pussy willow. It grows in damp or swampy places and before the leaves come out in the spring the "pussies" are seen on the branches. They are little, soft, silvery pussies, and it is not everybody who knows what they really are.

Each "pussy" or catkin, as we must call it, is a group of small flowers, or rather flower-buds, for after the flowers are fully out the pussies lose their soft, silky appearance and no longer deserve to be called pussies.

Pussy willow

Staminate catkin fully out

The older catkins are covered with stamens full of yellow pollen or else with seed pods. For willows bear two kinds of flowers, the stamen-bearing, or staminate flowers, and the seed-bearing, or pistillate flowers.

The staminate flowers grow on one willow tree, and the pistillate ones on another.

The pollen in the staminate flowers is very abundant and is carried by the wind or by insects to the pistillate flowers. If you shake a twig of ripe staminate catkins, your hands and clothes will be covered with pollen dust.

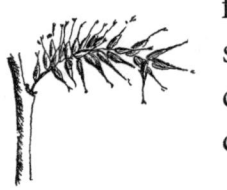
Pistillate catkin

Bees are fond of willow pollen and eagerly gather it in the early spring. The willow catkin has a tiny drop of nectar at the base of each little flower, and bees and flies are fond of this and visit the willows to get it. Of course, as the insects fly from one catkin to another, they carry pollen from one to another.

After a time the staminate flowers wither and fall, but the pistillate ones are followed by seed pods, and the stem that bears them lengthens to make room for the growing pods, and at last when the seeds are ripe the pods split open and out come the *tiniest* of little seeds, each with a tiny plume of down, and away they fly.

There are a great many species of willow, and not all of them are as pretty as the pussy willow. One reason why the pussy willow is so pretty is that the catkins appear before the leaves. In some willows the catkins come with the leaves, and in some they come after the leaves are fully grown. Many willows have bright red or yellow or green stems that give color to the landscape even in midwinter.

THE WILLOW

In all willows the pistillate catkins bear pods that open and let out fluffy seeds.

Ripe willow catkin

The cottonwood trees are relatives of the willows. Their seeds are so very downy that when they are ripe the ground beneath the trees will often be white, as though a light snow had fallen.

It is because the seeds are so abundantly supplied with soft cottony plumes that the tree is called cottonwood.

Poplars are also closely related to the willows and, like them, have fluffy seeds.

In the early summer, if you look in the right place, you will see plenty of them.

Willow and poplar twigs are very strong and limber, and some kinds are used to make baskets and chairs and cradles and a great many other useful things. The slender young twigs are woven together and make very strong and durable articles.

Since only the long twigs can be used, people get them in large quantities by cutting off the heads of the trees, when long sprouts shoot up all around the ends of the cut limbs. Cutting off the tops of the trees in this way is called pollarding, and a pollarded willow or poplar is rather a funny sight, particularly after it has had its head cut off a number of times.

Willow branches about as large around as one's

Pollarded willows

finger make very good whistles in the spring of the year. The sap flowing under the bark loosens it, so that by pounding the twig the bark can be slipped off unbroken, the wood beneath cut as desired, and the bark slipped on again.

The dotted lines show how the wood should be cut away under the bark.

Willow twigs also make very good switches, and long, ah, very long ago, when children used to be naughty, willow switches were in great demand.

In these later days children are never naughty I suppose—or is it only that switching has gone out of fashion?

These switches did not come from weeping willows, though that certainly would have been a very appropriate name for them.

THE WILLOW

Weeping willows are large and beautiful trees that came from the eastern part of Asia. The twigs are very long and slender and hang down like a veil all about the tree.

Weeping willows are favorites in parks and pleasure grounds, and it used to be the fashion to plant them in cemeteries, at the heads of gravestones.

Everybody who has tried to preserve bird skins, or the skins of small animals, doubtless knows what salicylic acid is, but not everybody knows that this is obtained from the bark of willows and poplars. Some species of willow contain a great deal of the substance from which salicylic acid is made.

Salicylic acid prevents animal tissue from decaying, and it is also used as a medicine. It is not poisonous, but is rather unpleasant to handle, as it is apt to make one sneeze.

The bark of willows is also used in Europe for tanning, instead of oak or hemlock bark, which is commonly used in this country.

"Tan bark" is bark that has been ground up and had the "tannin," or substance that hardens leather, extracted from it. The tan bark is then put on roads or walks, or sometimes on city streets, to deaden the noise. It is often used in the country for banking up houses in the winter.

Willows grow quickly, and some of those that like wet places are often planted on sandy shores of lakes or streams, or on banks, that their roots may bind the sand or loose earth together and so keep the shore from shifting.

Very often a willow twig, can be made to grow by merely sticking the cut end in damp earth, and many a large willow has thus been planted as a twig by the hand of a little child.

CATTAILS

Cattails in bloom

Cattail seeds fly, too! It is surprising to know that cattails blossom. But they do.

In the early spring, cattails look green instead of brown, and the thickened green part near the top is made of very, very small flowers packed tightly together.

The brown velvety part of the cattail succeeds the green flowers, and is but a collection of tiny seed pods that fluff out with tiny plumes in the autumn.

There are two kinds of flowers in cattails, as there are in willows, only in the cattails the two kinds are on the same plant. If you look at a cattail in its green stage, you will easily find the staminate flowers growing at the very top of the stalk,— at *A* in the picture. Out of these staminate flowers you can shake clouds of yellow pollen. Below the staminate flowers at *B* are the pistillate flowers, very small and packed very closely together. Each one has a seed pod at its base, and each seed pod when ripe has a tiny plume.

Of course the seed pods fly away on the wings of the wind. Being so small and light, they are sometimes carried a long distance.

A good many, no doubt, are so unfortunate as to fall on dry ground, and that is the end of them.

Cattails with ripe seeds

But others fall in swamps and ditches, where they grow vigorously and often fill up the swamp or the ditch so that it becomes a bed of cattails.

The downy cattail seeds are gathered in some places and made into mattresses for people to sleep on.

GERANIUMS

The bright flowers raised in hothouses or in windows, and that we call geraniums, do not often bear seed in the house.

In that part of the world where they grow wild, and out of doors in the summer time, they do. And their seeds are very curious indeed; for they can not only fly about but can bury themselves in the ground.

The geranium flower bears five curious seed pods that grow close together around a common center. Each seed pod has one seed, and when the seed is ripe the pod splits away from the center-piece. The pod runs up to a point, as you can see in the picture.

There is a long feather-

LITTLE WANDERERS

like plume packed in the long stem-like part of the pod, and this comes out when the pod splits away. Then the whole thing is floated off by the wind. This curious plume curls up like a corkscrew when dry, and so pushes the seed down into the grass or the earth where it has fallen. When the plume is made damp by rain or dew it straightens out.

At the bottom of the seed case are a few hairs or bristles that point backward and hold the seed so that it cannot be pulled out of the ground when the plume curls and straightens, but must always be pushed farther in.

It is a good plan for every one who has not seen the geranium seed case try to plant itself, to gather some ripe seeds and lay them on the earth in a flower pot. Let them get dry, then moisten them, then let them become dry again, and so on, until one has seen just how they work.

COTTON

"Down South" are a great many cotton fields. Cotton was brought to the United States from China and other far-away places. It did not find its way here accidentally with other seeds, like the dandelions and Canada thistles, but was brought on purpose and carefully cultivated.

A cotton field in early summer is rather a pretty sight. It is covered with light green little plants in straight rows; they have pretty leaves and yellowish flowers that soon turn red. These flowers are about the size of a morning-glory.

Ripe cotton bolls

In the fall a cotton field is much more interesting. Then the cotton plants are three or four feet high and have branched out into quite large bushes. The leaves have withered, but the bushes are covered with cotton bolls, or pods, out of which are bursting quantities of snowy white cotton. The field looks as if a skyful of soft little snowballs had fallen upon it.

An unopened boll (½ nat. size)

The cotton flowers are succeeded by pods, or bolls as they are called, and these contain black seeds about the size of a white bean. Each seed when ripe wears a coat of long, soft, white cotton fibers, and when the bolls split open to let out the seeds, out gush streams of snowy cotton. A cotton field is most picturesque during the picking season, when the negroes, the women with bright kerchiefs over their heads, go into the fields, pick the cotton, and carry it away in large baskets.

Each cotton seed is covered with cotton fiber that clings very close and has to be removed by machinery. The machine that does this is called a cotton gin, and is a very interesting and wonderful machine.

A boll just opened (½ nat. size)

Cotton seeds are cleaned more than once; the first time the long fibers are pulled off, and this is the best of the cotton. Then the seeds are cleaned again of less valuable, because shorter, fibers, and finally of the short fuzzy coat that clings to them after the second cleaning. The result of the last cleaning is a very inferior cotton, used only for a few kinds of cheap cloth.

Not all cotton has white fiber. The Nankin cotton,

which is grown near the mouth of the Mississippi River in this country, is naturally of a light tan color.

Cotton is one of the most useful plants in the world, and a great deal of attention is given to raising and manufacturing it.

The cotton has to go through a good many processes before it is finally ready to be spun into thread and then woven into cloth.

Some very useful cotton is not spun into thread, but comes to us in clean, soft rolls, which we call cotton batting. This is useful for many household purposes, and when very thoroughly cleaned is used by doctors in dressing wounds.

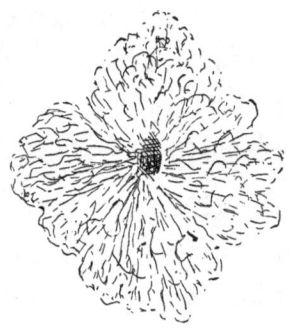

A seed and its coat of cotton

A large part of our clothing is made from the cotton that grows on the seeds of the cotton plant. The plant did not make the cotton for us, but probably to enable its seeds to be carried away by the wind and firmly fastened to the ground, when they lodged there. For a cotton seed clings very tightly to the earth, particularly after it has been wet.

Cotton seeds are very useful aside from the cotton they are clothed with. They contain a good deal of oil and are ground in mills, that the oil may be pressed out. This oil is put to a number of uses, and when purified is even used instead of olive oil as food. The meal that is left after the oil has been pressed out makes a valuable fertilizer, and is also used as food for cattle. Horses will not eat it, but cows are so fond of it that they will come long distances to the mills in order to lick up what meal they can find. This is the way its value as a food for cattle was discovered.

Cotton-seed meal is bright greenish yellow in color, and as it colors everything it touches, the cotton-seed mills are rather picturesque to look at, though not very pleasant to walk about in.

The bark of the root of the cotton plant is used as a medicine. But though so many parts of this wonderful plant are useful, the cotton that covers the seeds is the most valuable of all.

OTHER FLY-AWAYS

A GREAT many other plants have plumed seeds, and some have seeds with cottony coats, but of all the cotton-covered seeds those of the cotton plant are the only ones with fibers long and strong enough to be spun and woven.

It would be useless to try to tell about all the fly-away seeds. There are so many of them one would never get through. But it is great fun to discover them for ourselves. If we watch through the summer, we shall find many and many of them.

Quite a number of the grasses have plumes to their seeds, and some of these plumed grasses are very pretty indeed. We often see them used to decorate houses, and in Florida one can see very beautiful grass plumes growing in swamps. Everywhere the fields and woods

Fireweed

are full of seed wanderers that fly about to find a home, and all that any one need do who wants to see these pretty things is to look about and find them.

SEEDS THAT FLY WITH WINGS

MAPLES

MAPLE seeds also fly, but they have no silky or feathery or cottony plumes. They have wings instead. The fruit of the maple tree is called a samara and consists of a seed pod with a wing. Usually two pods grow together, though when thoroughly dry they fall apart.

The wings are thin and light, and the wind sometimes carries them a long distance. The maple blooms in the spring or early summer, and though its flowers have only stamens or pistils and no bright petals, yet they are very pretty.

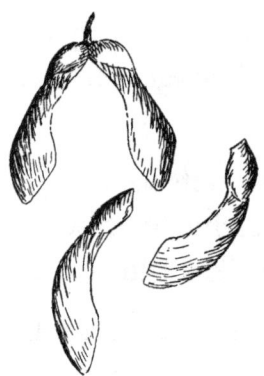

Maples, like willows and cattails, often have two kinds of flowers. One maple tree will often have all staminate flowers, and will look as if trimmed with fringe, as the staminate flowers have slender stems like threads.

The red maple, which blooms early in the spring before its leaves come out, has bright red fringes.

Sometimes these red-flowered trees bloom in January, in Florida, when the trees and bushes around them are bare, and you can imagine they make the swamps where they grow look very bright.

The pistillate flowers are not quite as airy as the staminate ones, but still they make pretty fringes upon the trees.

The wind blows the pollen from the staminate flowers to the pistillate ones growing on neighboring trees, and that is why the flowers hang out on long stems.

Some maples have green fringes and some have yellow ones, but all are beautiful.

After the flowering season is over, the staminate flowers disappear. But the pistillate flowers are followed by clusters of samaras, which are sometimes almost as bright in color and as pretty as the flower fringes.

When the samaras are ripe, they fall from the tree and are blown about by the wind. They cannot fly as far as the plumed seeds, but they sometimes get carried quite a distance.

The seed within the samara often sprouts soon after it falls. You can see little maple trees starting to grow by the roadside, or even along city sidewalks or in lawns.

The samaras of the early flowering maple trees fall quite early in the summer, but there are other maples whose samaras remain on the trees until autumn.

MAPLES

Maples make beautiful shade trees, and some species grow to a large size. One of the largest and most beautiful of them is the sugar maple, which is not only valuable as a shade tree, but yields delicious maple syrup from its sap.

The bark of this tree is "tapped," that is, a hole is bored through it into the wood beneath, early in the spring, and a little wooden tube or trough is driven into the hole. A pail is hung or set beneath to catch the sap as it runs out. Sap runs best when the days are warm and the nights cold; then there are merry times in the sugar camps.

The sap is collected in large kettles and boiled to syrup, or until it hardens into sugar. Just before it is ready to turn to sugar, it makes delicious "wax." You pour the hot, thick syrup upon snow, and when it thickens into a sticky paste you eat it. It is better than any kind of candy—at least I think so.

A great deal of sugar is made in the New England States, where the maple grows abundantly, and in the early days the only sugar some of the people had was maple sugar.

Sometimes the sap of other trees, as birches or elms, is made into syrup, but none is as abundant or as good as the maple syrup.

The wood of the sugar maple is hard and is valuable for furniture and other uses. Indeed the wood of most of the maples is prized for furniture making.

The bird's eye maple is a very pretty satiny wood dotted over with round spots that look a little like eyes. It comes from certain sugar maples whose wood is full of little knotty places.

The curled maple is also a pretty wood with wavy, shining lines made by irregular streaks in the wood. It is sometimes found in sugar maples and sometimes in other maples. Maple wood is light in color, and the bark of the tree is rather smooth. It is gray in most species, and often has white spots on it.

ELMS

The American elm is one of the most beautiful trees in the world, it is so majestic in size and so graceful in form.

If you do not know the elm tree, get some one to point it out to you at once, and you will feel that you have made a new friend. It is a very good thing to make friends with the trees and to learn to know them when you see them.

Elm trees have winged seed pods or samaras. The trees are covered with pretty, short fringes in the springtime—very pretty, but not as airy and pretty as the maple fringes. The pistillate flowers are followed by samaras that do not grow two together, and that have the wing growing around them instead of from one end.

The bark of the elm is very handsome;

it is marked quite regularly and is easy to recognize. It is a good thing to learn to know a tree by its bark. The bark of trees is an interesting and beautiful subject for study.

The wood of the elm is tough and hard, and is used in building ships and making wheels, and for other purposes where a tough, hard wood is required.

There are a number of species of elm trees, but the best-known one is the beautiful American elm that is everywhere used in parks and for shade trees. Next to this is the red elm, or slippery elm, whose inner bark is fragrant and mucilaginous and good to chew. This bark is good for colds and is sometimes ground up and made into lozenges.

Every country boy lays up a supply of slippery elm bark to dry in the attic along with his nuts.

ASH TREES

Ash trees are tall, straight, and handsome, with a very dark-colored bark, so regularly marked that one soon learns to know it at a glance. I once knew three of them that stood in an open pasture on the shore of Lake Ontario.

It was worth going to the pasture in a high wind to see the tall, beautiful trunks sway as the wind struck them. I used to wish I could climb up into the tops of them, though it would have been a very unsafe perch indeed.

You have guessed by now that ash trees have winged seed pods, and so they have.

When the little clusters of ash flowers first show in the springtime they are black, and the tree seems to have black-tipped branches. Soon the black tips develop

into dark green fringes, though these are not airy and light, like the maple and elm fringes.

The best way for you to find out just how ash blossoms look is—but you know perfectly well what is the very best way to find out, and I hope you will take care to do it.

Ash samaras

Ash seeds are winged like those of the maples and are called samaras, but they do not grow two together. Ash trees often bear great numbers of samaras, more than any other tree. Where ash trees grow near houses, the samaras often fall on the roofs and fill up the gutters, so that they have to be cleaned out, sometimes more than once in a season.

The wood of the ash is so very tough and elastic that from all time it has been used to make bows and spear shafts. Of course it is also valuable for less warlike uses.

When you read the "One Hoss Shay," you will find one use to which ash wood is sometimes put.

The ash tree used to be held sacred by the ancient Norsemen, and some day you will read beautiful stories about the wonderful ash Ygdrasil.

The small tree we call "mountain ash" is not an ash at all, and it has, as you know, red berries instead of samaras.

PINES

PINE trees bear cones, and cones do not fly. But if you examine the scales of the cones, you will find a winged seed under each. When the cones are ripe the scales open and the seeds drop out and are caught by the wind and floated away.

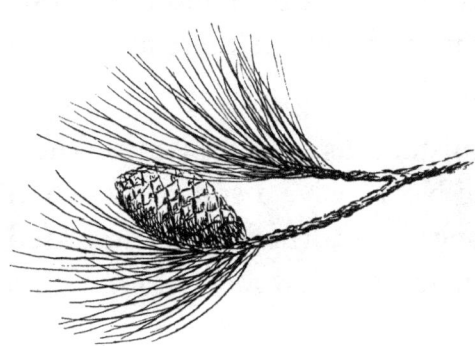

There are a great many species of pine trees. The seeds of some are large and sweet and are sold as pine nuts. These trees do not grow in this country, however, and we should have to go to South America, or to Asia, or western Europe to find pine trees from which we could gather nuts.

Squirrels gather nuts from all the pine trees, however, for they are not as particular as we, and think them all good. They are very clever at gathering cones, gnawing off the scales and getting out the seeds.

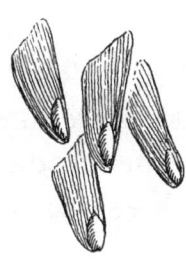

LITTLE WANDERERS

Pine trees, like the maples and elms, have two kinds of—not exactly flowers, but something answering to them. The ovules, or young seeds, are borne under the scales of the cones, and the stamens are in catkins. Sometimes these catkins are very large, and they bear a great deal of pollen which the wind carries to the cones.

A pine forest is always a sweet and delightful place. When the sun shines on the trees they fill the air with fragrance.

Pine trees used to grow all over the northern part of the United States, but they make very valuable timber, and so have been carelessly cut down and the forests destroyed, until now in many places there are almost no pine trees left.

This was a great mistake, as the people now know. The white pine of the North gave a soft white wood that could be easily carved or "turned," and it was used more extensively than any other wood as long as the forests lasted.

A large part of the South is still covered by forests of yellow pine, whose wood is dark, hard, and valuable for building purposes.

The pine forests of the South also yield large quantities of tar, resin, and turpentine, and it is sad to see the forests being carelessly destroyed each year. The trees are cut for their sap, from which turpentine and other products are made, but if the same trees are cut three years in succession they die.

PINES

The turpentine makers, however, cut them as long as they will yield sap, because it is easier to stay in one place three years than to move their camps to a region of fresh trees. This is wrong, and will result in destroying the valuable Southern pine forests in a short time.

We should take care of the trees, for they are our good friends. Besides providing wood for all sorts of uses, they protect the earth, keep it moist, and prevent the streams from drying up. In many places the farming land has been destroyed, because the forests were cut down when the land all about dried up, so that nothing of value to man could grow on it.

With proper management trees can be cut for use without destroying the forests.

SEEDS THAT FLY WITHOUT WINGS OR PLUMES

Poppy seeds have no wings and no plumes, and yet they are carried far and wide by the wind. That is because they are so very small and so very light. They look more like dust than seeds.

The poppy pod is like a cup with a cover on, but around the edge, just below the cover, is a row of small holes, each covered by a lid. These lids do not open until the poppy seeds are ripe; then they do, and the fine seeds can get out of the holes. But *how* do they get out? They cannot move of themselves, but the wind sways the poppy pod this way and that on its long stalk, and the little seeds are shaken out only to be caught by the wind and blown away.

Perhaps you think that is not a very sure way for the seeds to escape, but if you examine

Poppy pod

a poppy head that has been ripe for some time you will find scarcely a seed in it, so it proves to be a better way than it looks.

Nature's way is generally the best way to accomplish an object.

Poppies are often seen growing by the roadside or in the garden, far from the flower beds; that is because the wind has blown the seeds to these places.

In England the wheat fields are often gay with scarlet poppies, which have, no doubt, been sown with the wheat. They are beautiful to look at, though the farmer does not enjoy seeing them in his wheat.

Opium is obtained from the juice of the partly ripened seed pods of some kinds of poppies. Opium is very valuable as a medicine, but it has to be used with great care, as it is also a powerful poison.

A valuable oil is expressed from the seeds of the opium poppy. This oil is used for illuminating purposes in some parts of the world, and also for soap-making. The finer quality is used as food, instead of olive oil, in countries where oil is eaten instead of butter, and it is also used in grinding artists' colors.

OTHER SEEDS THAT ARE MOVED BY THE WIND

MANY, many other plants have seeds or seed pods that can be carried away by the wind. The fields and hedges are full of plumes and winged seeds, and of seeds so light as to be readily carried away without special plumes or wings.

At the top of this page is the picture of a trumpet vine. When you have the chance, examine the seeds in the pod of the trumpet vine and see how they are enabled to fly away.

Hops are pretty plants, and useful ones as well, and if you examine hop seeds—you will see—what you will see!

Some clovers have seeds that fly. See if you can find them.

Linden trees are covered with clusters of white sweet-scented flowers in the early summer. Each cluster of flowers is attached in a curious way to a wing, and

OTHER SEEDS THAT ARE MOVED BY THE WIND

often the whole cluster, with its wing, falls together and is blown to some distance by the wind. When the lindens are in bloom you will know it by the humming of the bees, for they are very fond of linden honey, and the trees often sound like an enormous beehive, there are so many bees about them.

It would take altogether too long to tell about all the seeds that are carried by the wind, but you can find a great many of them without being told; and that, after all, is the best way. At the bottom of this page are the seed pods of the cow parsnip, a very large, coarse, but rather handsome weed, often found in the corners of pastures. You can see that its seed pods fly.

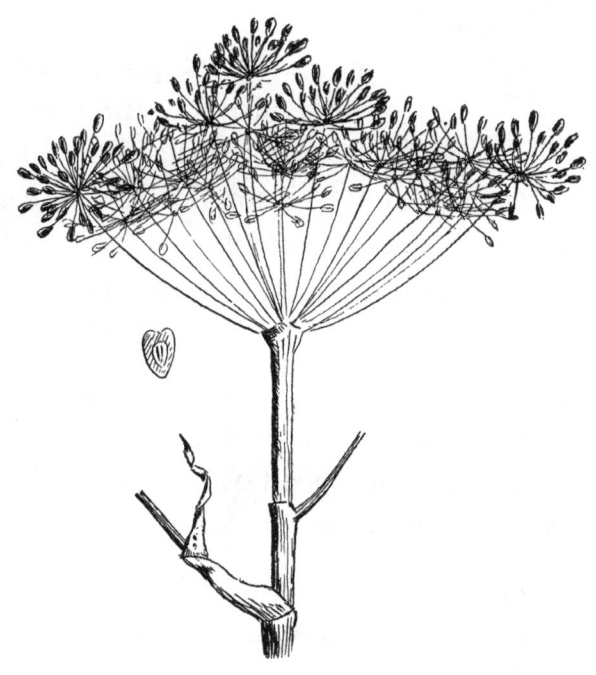

TUMBLEWEEDS

Tumbleweeds *are* funny! They do not fly in the air, but they go scurrying over the surface of the earth. They grow on the Western plains and in other places, and sometimes get to be as large as a bushel basket.

They are not very interesting until they begin to tumble. This happens in the fall of the year.

The plants grow like ordinary little bushes in the summer and bear a great many clusters of small flowers. Late in the season the leaves fall off, and the stems of the plant curl over and make a ball of it. The seeds do not fall yet; they can be seen in pretty brown clusters inside the ball.

Along comes a gust of wind; the tumbleweed, all rolled up and quite dry now, breaks loose from the earth and away it goes, head over heels, rolling like a wild thing across the prairies.

It is very funny to see a prairie full of tumbleweeds racing along. They look as if they were playing tag. When a train passes, those near the track are caught in the draught and off they start, head over heels, as fast

TUMBLEWEEDS

as they can. They look exactly as if they were chasing the train.

The tumbleweed does not send its seed children out alone into the world; it goes along and spills them over the prairies, as it tumbles about; for, after a while, the seeds get thoroughly ripe and fall off. If you were to see the tumbleweeds rolling about over the prairies in the fall, you would not wonder there are so many of them growing everywhere in the summer.

There are several kinds of tumbleweeds in the West. One of them is called the Russian thistle, though it is not a thistle. It came from Europe and has proved to be the very worst weed the farmer has to deal with.

It tumbles about in the fall, rolling far and wide over the prairies before the high winds. In a few years it has become such a nuisance that large sums of money are spent by the government to exterminate it. In some places the school children have been taught to recognize it and to pull it up wherever they see it growing.

WANDERERS THAT CLING

BURDOCKS

SEEDS have other ways of going about besides being blown by the wind. One way is to fasten on to anything or anybody that passes and get carried to some other place.

Burdocks do this. Burdocks grow in dooryards if they get a chance, and in fence corners and pastures and along roadsides, and in fact almost anywhere. They are sturdy weeds and often grow quite large. In "The Ugly Duckling," Hans Andersen tells us about them.

"In a sunny spot stood a pleasant old farmhouse, circled all about with deep canals; and from the walls down to the water's edge grew great burdocks, so high that

BURDOCKS

under the tallest of them a little child might stand upright."

Like the dandelions and Canada thistles, the burdocks came from Europe, and a great many people wish they had stayed at home. That is because of their burrs, which are a nuisance in the fall of the year.

Everybody knows what burrs are. They stick fast to the clothes of people and get on the tails and manes of horses, where they must cause a great deal of discomfort, and where it is a great deal of work to pick them out. They get upon the tails of cows, too, and the fleeces of sheep, and dogs get them on their ears. The reason is this: the burrs are full of seed pods. The burdock flower head is, like the dandelion, made up of a great many tiny flowers, and each flower has a close-fitting pod containing one seed, or an akene, as we have learned to call it.

The head of flowers is covered by stiff green bracts, and at the end of each bract is a hook. These hooks are soft when the flowers are in blossom, and they do not catch fast to things. But when the seeds ripen, the bracts grow hard and stiff, and so do the hooks at the end.

Now, when an animal or a person comes along and brushes against these ripe burrs, the strong hooks catch; the burr, full of ripe akenes, is pulled from the plant and is carried away. It is easy to guess why this happens.

When one tries to pull a ripe burr from the clothes, it falls all to pieces and the akenes spill out. Then each hook has to be pulled out separately, and very likely each one will prick the fingers.

Children sometimes pick the burrs before they are ripe, and stick them together to make baskets and other things. Then the burrs do not fall to pieces nor prick the fingers much. The burdock has a rank, disagreeable odor that clings to the fingers a long time after the burrs have been handled. It is not easy even to wash it off.

Children often pick ripe burrs and throw them at each other. Some think this is funny, and some think it is naughty.

Burdocks yield a valuable medicine; so they are useful as well as troublesome.

COCKLEBURS AND SAND SPURS

Cockleburs are covered with hooks, too, but they are much uglier than burdocks, for their seed pods are very hard and are covered on the outside with stiff, strong hooks that prick like needles.

When one walks among cockleburs, he soon stops to pick them off, for they hurt so, he cannot bear it.

Sand spurs are even worse than cockleburs. They are the seed coverings to a kind of grass.

In Florida this grass grows in tufts and spreads out close to the ground. Some of its stalks are covered with sand spurs that, like the cockleburs, are hard and are covered, not with hooks, but with very hard spines.

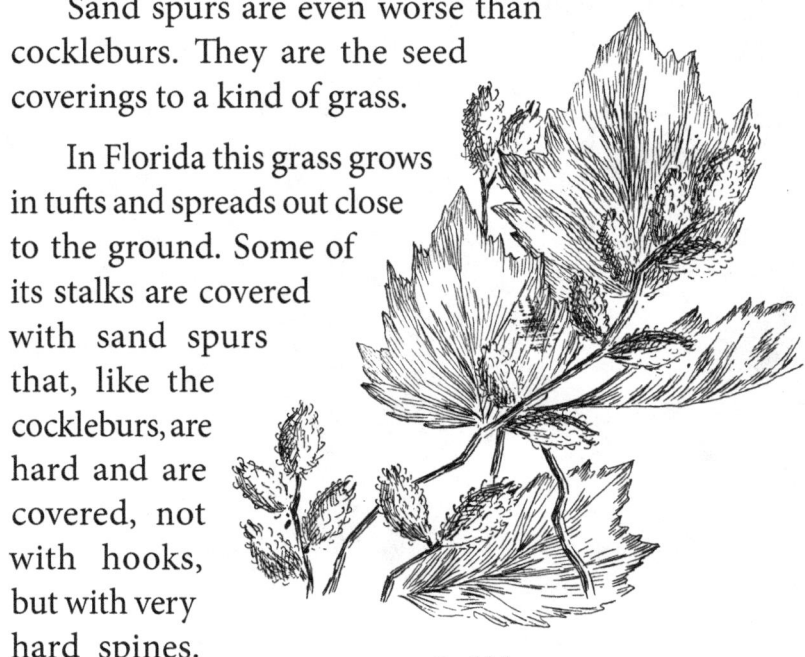

Cockleburs

LITTLE WANDERERS

These spines stick out in all directions and readily fasten upon whomever or whatever comes along, when they leave the parent grass and are carried away. After a time they are picked off and thrown on the ground, or they fall off, and that is their way of traveling to find a place to grow.

Dogs often get them in their feet, and then they have a hard time picking them out, for of course the poor things cannot walk with sand spurs between their toes.

There was once a dog that hated sand spurs and loved people so much that when any one came near him with sand spurs on his clothes, he would at once begin to pick them off, and the expression with which he jerked them out of his mouth showed very plainly what he thought of sand spurs.

Sand spurs

TICK TREFOIL

When walking in the woods in the late summer we sometimes find queer jointed little pods, like unfinished pea pods, clinging to our clothes. These come from plants that belong to the Pea family and are called Tick Trefoil. There are nearly two dozen kinds of them, and sometimes they seem to be everywhere in the woods and thickets.

The pods are like pea pods, only that they are jointed, and the joints break apart, so that each may be carried away separately. Each joint contains a little pea-like seed.

The outside of the pod seems fuzzy, and it clings very closely to whatever it touches. If we look at the fuzz with a magnifying glass, we shall find it made up of innumerable little hooks.

The hairs that cover the pod are turned up at the end to form little hooks, very delicate, but able, when there are so many of them, to hold on very tightly.

They seem to snuggle down into the cloth they touch, so that it is difficult to pick them off, and the joints all separate when we try to remove them, so that each one has to be taken off separately.

Another plant whose seed pods are covered with hooked hairs is the sweet-scented bedstraw. This is a pretty little plant that spreads about on the ground. Its flowers are small and greenish, but the whole plant when in bloom has a pretty lace-like effect as we find it in the woods very often growing about fallen logs.

Sweet-scented bedstraw

Its seed pods are small and, like the tick trefoil, are covered with hairs that, under the magnifying glass, are seen to be hooked.

The enchanter's nightshade is another little plant whose seed pods are covered with hooked hair. It is as pretty as its name and is to be found in damp woods.

There is a tall leafy kind that grows sometimes two feet high and is topped with numerous branches of small white flowers. As the flower stem lengthens, the flowers continue to unfold at the tip, while lower down

TICK TREFOIL

are the many little seed pods, shaped like little tennis racquets.

The prettiest enchanter's nightshade, however, is a little fairy that sometimes grows on decaying logs. It is often not more than three or four inches high and ends in a branch of pretty little white flowers with bright red calyx lobes. After these dainty blossoms come the little hook-haired, racquet-shaped seed pods.

Look for enchanter's nightshade the next time you go to the woods in the summer time. Below is a picture of the large one.

STICK-TIGHTS

STICK-TIGHTS are troublesome to us, and we call them very disagreeable names, such as beggar ticks and beggar lice. But they are really not bad at all and are quite pretty. If they stick to us, that is our fault quite as much as theirs, for we should keep away from them if we are unwilling to carry them about.

They cling to whatever comes along, because that is their way of traveling about. They cannot walk or creep or crawl or jump; neither can they fly very far nor move in any other way, excepting as they are carried.

You know how they look—so little brown, flat object with horns. Of course this is an akene. Inside it is a seed. The two horns at the top are able to fasten it quite tightly to a woolen dress or a sheep's fleece. If you look carefully, you will see little hard teeth on the edge of the stick-tight that help it to cling. On one species of stick-tight these teeth point backward, like the barbs of a fishhook, and that kind sticks very tightly.

Stick-tight plants blossom in the summer time. The greenish-yellow flowers are clustered in heads like the dandelion flowers, and like those each stick-tight flower has an akene at the bottom. These akenes grow much

STICK-TIGHTS

larger than those of the dandelion, and they have the two horns on their heads.

The akenes stand on a flat cushion, just as the dandelion akenes do, but these do not wait for the wind to blow them away, though, if nothing comes along to pull them loose, they in time become very dry and fall out, and then the wind often carries the light little things some distance.

Stick-tight plant

But their favorite method of traveling is by stagecoach, and if you happen along at the right time they will take you for their stagecoach, and let you carry them to a new place. Sometimes the plants grow so closely together that in passing through them one becomes quite covered with the little brown things, and it is a long and tiresome task to pick them out.

They, too, get on the tails and manes of horses, and the tails of cows, the coats of dogs, and the fleeces of sheep; but they are not nearly as troublesome to these creatures as are the burdocks.

There are several species of stick-tights, or beggar ticks, as they are more generally called.

Some have rather large flower heads, with the outer flowers each provided with a long, broad yellow petal.

These are often called wild sunflowers, because they look something like a little sunflower.

There is a plant called Spanish needles, very closely related to the stick-tights, and that has four horns to its seed pod.

The burr marigold, which grows in wet places, and whose greenish flower heads are round like a marble, is also related to the stick-tights, and, like the Spanish needles, has four horns.

A great many plants have these little horned seed cases, and when you go about the country in the fall of the year you will be certain to make the acquaintance of some of them. The plants with horned seed pods wish their seeds to get out of the dense thickets in which they usually grow, and they do what they can to help them.

AGRIMONY AND OTHER WEEDS

In the fall of the year and towards the end of summer we find a great many weeds in the woods and along the roads, sending their seeds out into the world by means of stout hooks, or else hooked hairs or sharp spines.

The agrimony is one of these. It is a common, rather pretty plant with yellow flowers, and it has a burr or seed pod, armed with hooked prickles around the waist, so to speak.

After a walk in the country through woods and fields, in the autumn, one will be likely to find a number of little things clinging to one's clothes. Instead of merely shaking or picking them off and throwing them away, carefully collect them, and when there is time look at them. You will very likely find yourself decorated with a number of different kinds of seeds or seed pods, that vainly hoped in you to

LITTLE WANDERERS

find a means of traveling to new and better places of growth.

All these little brown things are disappointed, or would be if they could feel disappointed. But you can profit by their misfortune, and, by carefully examining the little wanderers, can learn a great many interesting and wonderful truths about the plant world in its effort to scatter its seeds.

FLAX

THE flax is a very useful plant, for the fibers of its stems are long and strong, and are spun into thread and then woven into linen.

Besides this, the seeds are useful. They contain an oil which is pressed out and is known as linseed oil. It is used a great deal by painters in mixing their paints.

When flaxseeds are wet they become very sticky on the outside. A jelly-like substance covers them, and this it is which we drink in "flaxseed tea" to cure our colds.

Flax

You can easily see this jelly-like covering by putting a few flaxseeds in a few drops of water and leaving them there a little while.

You can readily see that when the flaxseeds are shed in the field and are met by the rain, they would stick to the feathers, feet, and beaks of birds that came to eat the seeds. If the birds flew to another place, as they often would, to clean their plumage, they would rub off the flaxseeds, that meantime had become dry again, and often the seeds would drop off, as the bird moved about. In this way they would get planted in new places. No doubt the sticky covering to the wet seed also helps to anchor it to the ground and keep it from blowing away when once it has settled down on the earth.

The flax plant that we find so useful is not wild. It is carefully cultivated in many parts of the world and has been cultivated for so long a time, and in so many places, that nobody knows where it first came from. It is a pretty plant, that bears bright blue flowers.

Why do you not buy a penny's worth of flaxseeds at the drug store and plant them in your garden and become acquainted with this very interesting and beautiful little plant?

MISTLETOE

The mistletoe grows on trees. It has no roots of its own, but attaches itself to the bark of the tree and sucks out the sap.

Since it lives up in trees, its seeds must be able to find lodgment in these high places; and this the birds help them to do. The mistletoe has light green leaves; it grows in bunches and bears white berries.

The seeds in the berries are covered by a viscid substance, and when the birds eat the berries, some of these seeds will be apt to cling to them and be left on the branches of some other tree.

If the seeds happen to get swallowed, that does not hurt them, for they are not digested, but are passed out just as they were swallowed, and they then often fall upon the tree branches, where they can grow.

The English mistletoe very often grows upon the oak tree, and from very early times the plant was reverenced by the people, and particularly by the Druids, who used it in their religious observances. A survival of this old superstition about the mistletoe is found in its use to-day at Christmas time.

OTHER PLANTS WITH STICKY SEEDS OR SEED PODS

Quite a number of plants prepare sticky coverings to their seeds or seed pods, in order to help the seeds get away.

The squirting cucumber is one of the most curious of these. It grows wild in southern Europe, but is sometimes seen in gardens in this country, not because of its beauty, but because it is so curious. It is a hairy plant and not at all pretty, but when its hairy cucumber-shaped seed pods are ripe something funny happens. The pod falls from the vine, and through the round hole left when it fell away from its stem, that which is inside the pod is shot out with violence. Out fly seeds and a quantity of sticky liquid. If a bird happens to be about when this happens, he will make haste to get far from such a queer-acting plant; and if he was shot by it, he will carry some of the sticky seeds with him; or he may get the seeds attached to him after they have been shot out.

You see the squirting cucumber has two ways of

sending its seeds on their journey into the world. It shoots them some distance at the start and also provides them with a sticky covering, so that they may have a chance to get carried still farther.

Some plants have sticky hairs growing to their seed pods. We know that a good many plants have their pods covered with hairs which are hooked at the ends. Well, some are covered with hairs that have a drop of viscid substance at the tip, instead of a hook; these hairs fasten on quite as firmly as if they were hooked.

The pretty little twin flower, or ground vine, as it is sometimes called, has a pair of scales growing about its seed pod, and these scales are covered with sticky hairs.

The twin flower

The soft little mouse-ear chickweed, that grows everywhere in waste places, has several species which are covered all over with fine hairs which have a sticky tip. When the plant withers, it is easily pulled from the ground, and as it remains sticky, even after withering, the whole plant is often carried away by passing animals or people, and its seeds shed in some distant place.

See if you can find some plants that have their seeds carried because some part of the plant is sticky. There are not a great many of them; still, if you look long enough, you will be sure to find some.

WANDERERS THAT FLOAT

Some kinds of plants live in the water or on the edge of it. These often have seeds or seed pods light enough to float. You can generally see little seeds floating about on ponds, if you take the trouble to look.

Into these ponds come ducks or herons or other waterfowl. The birds come to find something to eat, and as they swim or wade about they come in contact with the wet seeds that cling to them. After a time the birds, bearing the seeds on plumage, beak, or feet, fly to another pond or marsh, and as they alight the seeds are floated off.

The wind then blows them to the shore, or else in time, if they live in the water, they sink to the bottom and sprout.

The cocoanut is a seed that is surrounded by a strong shell and a thick coat of fiber that protects it from the water and also makes it light.

The nut inside this thick overcoat is hollow when ripe, excepting for a watery liquid that we call the milk of the cocoanut. As we see cocoanuts in stores, the outer coat has been taken off.

Cocoanuts grow near the tops of tall cocoanut

palms, and these palms are fond of standing on the seashore. When the nuts get ripe they often fall in the sea and are carried long distances by the ocean currents. In this way, no doubt, many a coral island has received its lovely fringe of cocoanut palms.

The nuts are floated to these little islands and washed into crevices on them, where they lodge and in time grow into stately trees.

Cocoanut palms

The cocoanut palm is a very important tree in tropical countries. The nuts are used as food, and a valuable oil is obtained from them. Cocoa oil is used for illuminating and also for making salves.

The thick fiber that surrounds the nut is strong and tough and is made into cloth, matting, brushes, baskets, coarse rope, and a number of things. Matting is used in some hot countries to make the sides of houses, and the cocoanut fiber is useful to thatch roofs.

The wood of the tree is hard and durable and is made into many household articles. The hard shell of the nut makes good cups and dishes. So you see the cocoa-nut tree affords almost everything the people in the hot countries need.

WANDERERS THAT FLOAT

They make their houses and furnish them from it, they get food and drink from it, for the milk of the cocoanut is a very pleasant beverage, and they use the oil to light their abodes at night. No wonder the people value this noble tree very highly.

SEEDS THAT ANIMALS LIKE TO EAT

THE HICKORY

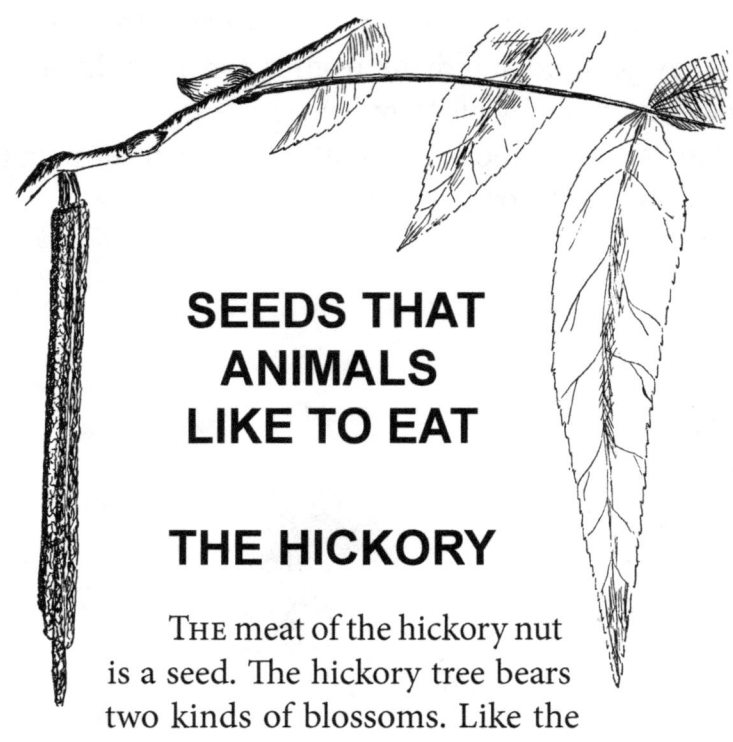

The meat of the hickory nut is a seed. The hickory tree bears two kinds of blossoms. Like the willow, it has staminate catkins and also bears pistillate flowers, from which grow nuts. Some hickory catkins are very long and slender and make pretty green tassels on the trees in the spring. Hickory nuts are good to eat, and you may wonder how these delicious nuts, that many creatures are fond of, ever get a chance to grow.

Squirrels are fond of nuts, and they are generally on hand when the nuts are ripe.

The green nuts have an outer covering that splits open when the nut is ripe and lets

Young hickory nuts

THE HICKORY

it fall to the ground. Of course when a squirrel has eaten a nut, that is the end of it. But squirrels are good housekeepers and store away nuts in holes in the trees or in the ground. Chipmunks do the same, and some birds, as nutcrackers and blue jays, hide nuts in the same way. Often these nuts are forgotten, or else the little creature that hid them may die or be killed. Then the nuts that have been put in the ground have nothing to do but grow when spring warms the earth.

You see they have been planted by the little nut lovers, that certainly had no intention of planting them. No doubt a great many nut trees get started in this way. Hickory nuts are often called "walnuts" in New England. The hickory tree belongs to North America, and before this continent was discovered only the Indians enjoyed hickory nuts. Now they are sent to England, and indeed all over the world.

The wood of the hickory is hard, tough, and flexible and is very valuable.

Andrew Jackson was called "Old Hickory" because of his unyielding nature, and when you study the history of the United States, or read the life of Jackson, you will not wonder that he was so named.

Hickory switches were used long ago when children were naughty; they were preferred to willow, because they did not break so easily.

A better use to put hickory to is to burn it. Hickory

logs make a very hot and beautiful fire, and hickory is one of the best of woods to burn in fireplaces.

WALNUTS AND BUTTERNUTS

BLACK walnuts grow on large, handsome trees of very hard, fragrant, dark-colored wood. Walnut wood used to be prized more highly than it is to-day for furniture and the inside finish to houses. It takes a fine polish but grows rather dark and somber-looking with age.

The black walnut is a native of the eastern part of North America. It belongs to the same family as the hickory and, like that, bears two kinds of flowers.

The nuts have hard, thick, black shells, and also a softer outer covering, or rind, that is very bitter and disagreeable to the taste, and that stains the fingers a dark brown.

Ripe walnuts

The "meat," or kernel, of the walnut is very oily, and some people do not like it because of its rather strong flavor. Squirrels are fond of walnuts, however, and often plant them in the way we have seen.

The English walnut is an Asiatic tree belonging to

the same family, which has been cultivated in Europe and, to a small extent, in this country. Its nut is larger than the black walnut, has a thin shell and a large, sweet kernel. The nut is delicious and a great favorite at Christmas time. It is sometimes picked green and pickled, and some people are very fond of pickled walnuts.

The nut yields an abundance of valuable oil, and the wood of the tree is very beautiful and useful for many purposes, one of which is to finish houses on the inside, and another to make gunstocks.

There is another tree belonging to the same family that grows in America and looks very much like the black walnut tree. It is the butternut. Butternut wood is valuable, and butternuts have sweet, oily kernels that most people like. The flowers, of course, are like those of the walnut.

Butternuts

A brown dye is made from the inner bark of the butternut tree, and also a medicine is obtained from it.

During the War of the Rebellion the Southern soldiers were often dressed in homespun clothes dyed by the bark of the butternut, and on this account they were called "butternuts."

THE CHESTNUT

THE chestnut is a very large and beautiful tree that grows abundantly in some parts of New England and over the Alleghany Mountains. Children always know the chestnut trees, if they live near them.

Like the hickory and walnut, the chestnut has its staminate flowers in catkins, but these are white instead of green, and give the chestnut a very handsome appearance when they cover it with airy plumes in the early summer.

Chestnut flowers

The nuts grow in prickly burrs, two or three in a burr. When the nuts are ripe in the fall, the burrs open to let them out. As everybody knows, they have a thin shell and a sweet kernel. They are sometimes boiled and sometimes eaten raw.

Squirrels, chipmunks, and some birds are fond of them and are often the means of planting them.

LITTLE WANDERERS

Chestnut wood is soft and has rather a coarse, loose grain. It is used largely for fence rails, cheap shingles, and railroad ties.

Chestnuts grow in some parts of Europe and Asia, and there is one kind that bears a nut as large as a black walnut. This nut is not as sweet as our chestnuts, but it is extensively used as food in some parts of Europe. The people go in families to gather the nuts, and prize them as we prize wheat and corn.

OTHER EDIBLE SEEDS

There are other nuts, as the pecan, whose tree belongs to the Hickory family and grows wild in the southern part of the United States; the beechnut, which grows on a stately tree of our forests; and the hazelnut, that grows on bushes in thickets near streams sometimes, or on the borders of woods.

But squirrels, chipmunks, birds, and such folk are not the only ones that plant seeds. Some ants do. Indeed ants are great hands to plant seeds. They do not take the hard nuts, but rather the seeds of certain grasses and other plants that bear rather small seeds. The ants carry the seeds into their holes, where they sometimes eat only one part of the seed, not enough to hurt it in the least, and so the seeds, buried in the ant-hills, are able to grow.

Hazelnuts

Ants often drop the seeds they are carrying and lose

them, and so the road to the home of the seed-eating ants is often grown over by plants the ants have sown.

Beechnut

BERRIES

SOME berries, such as raspberries and strawberries, are so good they seem to grow on purpose to be eaten. Very likely they do.

It is quite necessary for the blackberry and raspberry bushes to have their seeds sown at some distance from the parent plants, and it is also an advantage to strawberries to have their seeds dispersed. So what is better than to get the help of the birds?

To this end the berries are sweet and juicy when ripe, and they are bright in color, so that the birds can easily find them. A bird often picks a berry and carries it somewhere else to eat, and often it eats only a part and leaves the rest, which falls to the ground.

LITTLE WANDERERS

All berries have seeds in them or outside of them. Strawberries have the little seeds on the outside, as you can easily see.

Gooseberries, currants, and grapes have the little seeds inside, but, whichever way it is, some of the seeds will be left or scattered about by the birds that eat the berries. If some of the seeds are swallowed, that does not seem to hurt them; like the mistletoe seeds, they are able to sprout after having been eaten by a bird.

Birds eat a great many kinds of berries that we never think of eating. Notice how often in the late summer and the autumn you will see bright red or blue, or black, or white berries shining out from the leaves or bare branches of the wayside hedges. All of these are eaten by birds and carried away to new growing places.

Not all birds eat berries or seeds. Watch the birds and see if you can find out which kinds eat berries and seeds.

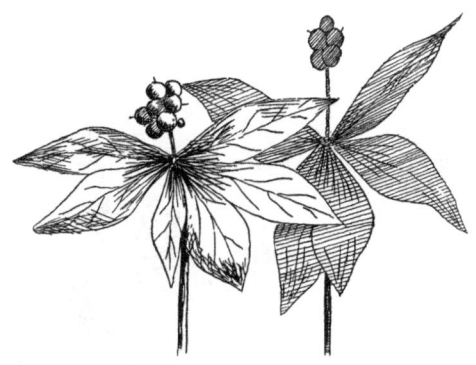

Bunchberries

CHERRIES

There is no need of describing cherries, as everybody knows them well.

The birds are so fond of ripe cherries that we sometimes have difficulty in getting our share before the robins and thrushes have taken all. Birds frequently fly away with the cherries, eat the pulp, and drop the stone, which, of course, contains a seed, and this seed then often sprouts and grows into a cherry tree. We sometimes find good cherries growing in hedges and thickets, far from the orchard; these have been planted there by the birds.

The sweet cherry is not a native of this country, but was brought here from Europe. We have a number of wild cherries, however, whose fruit we do not esteem, but the birds are fond of it, and they are the means of planting a good many wild cherry trees over the country.

Plums, peaches, and apricots are delicious fruits with hard-shelled seeds. The fruit is gathered, the pulp eaten, and the stone thrown away. We do not eat the seed of the plum, peach, and cherry, as we do that of the hickory and butternut. We throw it away, and thus disperse the seed children of these fruit trees.

The birds spread the seeds of the wild plums as they do those of the cherries. The kernels of all these seeds are bitter and contain a very poisonous substance.

Cherry trees have beautiful white blossoms that come early in the spring, and the peach trees have lovely pink blossoms. The peaches bloom the earliest of all, and as their flowers come out before the leaves, they turn the world into a maze of pink beauty in the parts where the peach orchards are.

Wild plum

APPLES

APPLES have tough cores in which their somewhat delicate seeds are protected. When we eat apples we throw the cores away. We now know that this is just what the apple wants.

If the core is tossed into a hedge by the roadside, its seeds may get a chance to sprout, and indeed they often do, for in the country we often come upon apple trees in out-of-the-way corners, where they were not planted by man on purpose.

Apples do not grow wild in this country, excepting crab apples. No doubt the birds carry away the ripe crab apples and drop the cores.

Pears and quinces have cores like the apples, and they are not natives of this country, but were brought here because of their delicious fruit. Sometimes we find them growing wild, and we know how this happened.

LITTLE WANDERERS

The next time we get a chance let us look for the fruit trees the birds have planted. There are a good many wild fruits that the birds are fond of, and whose seeds they are in the habit of dispersing over broad sections of country.

SEEDS THAT ARE SHOT AWAY

OXALIS

SOME plants have a way of shooting their seeds out of the pods. You know about the squirting cucumber. The little "sheep-sorrel," or yellow-flowered oxalis, that grows everywhere in the fields and gardens, has a way of shooting off its seeds when they are ripe.

There is an elastic covering over each seed, and when the pod opens, this covering splits and suddenly curls up, with force enough to send the seed quite a distance.

The leaves of the oxalis are sour, and children sometimes eat them.

Oxalis

A very powerful poison can be extracted from them, which is called oxalic acid, and sometimes salt of lemons, but there is not enough of this poison in the leaves to make them harmful to eat. The poison when obtained in large quantities is useful in the manufacture of calico, where it is used in printing the colors, and it is also sometimes used in a diluted form to clean metal work.

Be sure to look for the seed pods of the oxalis; they stand up like little candles and are very pretty. Gather some that are almost ripe and see how they shoot their seeds.

WITCH-HAZEL

This little tree blossoms in the fall of the year. After the leaves are gone, and sometimes after the snow has come, it stands in the edge of the woods dressed in a fairy costume of yellow lace-like flowers. After the flowers come the pods. They are very hard and horny and do not ripen until the next fall.

It is fun to gather ripe witch-hazel pods, for when they have been in the house a little while and have become thoroughly dry they "go off."

You may be sitting by the table reading, when pop!—a hard, shining little black seed strikes you in the face. It is the witch-hazel beginning its cannonade. Pop!—spat!—crack!—the battery has opened, and the seeds are flying with great force in all directions. They are sometimes shot several yards.

LITTLE WANDERERS

Of course in the woods this shooting is intended to start the seed children on their journey in the world.

The witch-hazel pod bursts open, and the edges turn in and press against the smooth seeds with great force, so that when they leave the pod they fly as though shot out of a sling. Get some witch-hazel pods and see how they do it.

Another name for witch-hazel is hamamelis, and from the bark is made a medicine which is put upon bruises. A forked twig of witch-hazel is sometimes used as a divining rod to find where to dig for water, or for gold or silver or other metals. The rod is held in the fingers of the diviner, who walks about, and wherever the rod turns and points down it is supposed to be the place to dig.

Divining rods are not much used in these days. People are not as superstitious, in some ways, as they used to be, and they know the rod cannot help them.

TOUCH-ME-NOT

THE touch-me-not, or snap-weed, is a delicate little plant that grows in wet places. Its yellow flowers are airily poised on slender stems, and the seed pods are very curious.

If one of them is touched, it goes off with a suddenness that is startling, until one gets used to it.

A pod that has snapped

When the pods are ripe they shoot the seeds out in all directions, and if you disturb a tangle of touch-me-nots in late summer you can hear the seeds popping on all sides.

There is a violet that shoots the seeds out of its pod, and the wild geranium pod slings its seeds to some distance by suddenly curling up on its long stalk.

A good many seed pods have this interesting habit,

but I doubt if you would discover that some peas and beans do this unless you were told.

The lupine, which belongs to the Pea family, shoots off its seeds by twisting the dry pod, as it opens to let them out. Even our garden sweet peas and some of our garden beans do this. Watch to see if you can catch them at it.

Plants have many, many ways of sending their precious seed children out in the world to find a growing place.

Lupine

There is no better way to spend our spare time than to watch the ripe fruits of plants and find out how the seeds are dispersed. Nearly all plants have some methods of sending their seeds abroad.

You will enjoy the plants more than ever when you begin to discover for yourself some of the things they do.

www.ingramcontent.com/pod-product-compliance
Lightning Source LLC
Chambersburg PA
CBHW031650040426
42453CB00006B/262